Quarter Horse Kids

An All-Around Rider

by

Jill Thomas

Foreword by Eugene "Geno" Spagnola

Written by Jill Thomas

Edited by Kendra Muntz

First edition February 2022

ISBN: 979-8-9853733-0-1

Note to readers: There is a glossary at the end of this book. Terms defined in the glossary are in type that looks like this on their first appearance.

This book is dedicated to Briella and Wyatt, without whose cooperation this book would not be possible. Special thanks also to Erin Ortega, Whitney Lagace, Gene Spagnola, Gretchen Mathes, and, of course, my husband Jeff Thomas for their support and input throughout the making of this book.

Foreword

by Eugene "Geno" Spagnola
Chairman, AQHA Professional Horsemen's Association

When Jill asked me to consider writing the foreword for this book, I started thinking about my career as a national level show competitor, horse trainer, and now, as the chairman of the AQHA Professional Horsemen's Association, and how those experiences might relate to a young rider like Briella.

My thoughts kept returning to the dozens of young students I've had the privilege of working with over my decades in the industry, and how many short- and long-term lessons those kids have learned by being involved in showing horses. Whether those riders competed locally or nationally, the horses they worked with and the experiences they had taught them so many lifelong skills that are valuable in every aspect of their lives today as adults. Young riders learn commitment, responsibility and compassion for themselves and another living being, and perseverance. They learn that hard work does count and that not everyone wins every time. They learn how to be good and unselfish winners as well as gracious and reflective losers.

What I particularly like about this book is that it's written by someone who has been involved with this aspect of AQHA, not only with her own child at the local level, but now as a national competitor herself. Jill has highlighted the values of showing that are almost intangible and yet perhaps the most important and the reason why so many people, young and old, love competing with their horses - doing just a bit better than the day before, the camaraderie of your barn friends, the satisfaction of being in sync with a 1200-pound animal through a pattern, the bonds you develop with your trainers, your fellow competitors and your horse, and so much more.

I'm so pleased to have had the opportunity to watch Briella develop over the last couple of years since she lives in my state, and I'm especially interested in watching her grow and become a team with her horse, Wyatt, who I had the pleasure of showing myself many years ago. I hope that other young people interested in showing horses find Briella's story to be informative AND inspirational, and that another generation of kids will dream big and ride strong.

An All-Around Rider

Hi! My name is Briella Ortega, and I'm 12 years old. I live in Connecticut, and this is my best friend, Wyatt. He is a **registered** American Quarter Horse, and we compete in American Quarter Horse Association (AQHA) horse shows. Some people may think riding horses is just fun and easy, but I'll tell you what—riding and showing Wyatt is hard work! There are a lot of ups and downs. But I love it and can't imagine doing anything else.

I've been riding horses—well, horses and ponies—since I was 4 years old. No one else in my immediate family rides right now, but my grandfather used to ride horses a long time ago. Maybe that's where my love of horses comes from. I started by riding a pony named Cheesy, and I performed some gymnastics on horseback. That's when you actually do handstands and other gymnastic moves on top of a moving horse while someone **lunges** the horse in a circle. I also competed in some small shows at my barn.

Then, just last year, my mom and dad gave Wyatt to me as a Christmas present. I may be the luckiest girl in the world! Now, Wyatt and I show in the AQHA **regiona**l and national **circuits** in the **novice** and **open** youth **all-around classes.**

So, let me tell you a little about Wyatt. First, Wyatt's registered name is *Platinum Sunsation*, but I just call him by his **barn name,** Wyatt. Since he's an American Quarter Horse, he needs to have a unique name to be officially registered to compete in the circuits. Some of the other horses' names sound pretty funny and are spelled funny, too, like *Whatscookingoodlookin* or *Best Day of the Week* or *Its Al Ways Sumthing.*

Wyatt is 17 years old and has been showing for longer than I've been alive! He has lots of experience, and he's teaching me how to be a great all-around rider for the AQHA shows I'm attending this year. He's a strong partner, and we're going to be a fantastic team.

The American Quarter Horse is the most popular **breed** in the United States. Of the 9.5 million horses in the U.S., 3.5 million of them are quarter horses. Quarter horses are a very versatile breed, and they can do just about anything: showing, rodeo, jumping, **cutting**, **reining**, **dressage**, **driving**, ranch work, and of course, racing. They were actually named quarter horses because they can run a quarter of a mile faster than any other horse breed. A **thoroughbred** horse, the ones that race in the Kentucky Derby, can run a longer distance faster than a quarter horse, but in a sprint, a quarter horse is the fastest.

In AQHA showing, some people specialize and compete in just one or two events like **western pleasure** or **hunter under saddle.** But Wyatt and I are all-around competitors, which means that we need to excel in both **English** and **western** classes as well as in different types of riding within each **discipline**. It takes a lot of hard work and determination to be a good all-around rider—and even more effort to be a competitive all-around horse.

Today, I ride at Whitney Ridge Stables. When I started riding there, I didn't have my own horse, so I rode a lot of different horses in my lessons. I also competed in YEDA, which stands for Youth Equestrian Development Association. In this competition, you ride a horse that doesn't belong to you and compete against other kids who come to your barn for the day. When you participate in YEDA, you earn points that count towards real money that the YEDA gives out to kids each year to use for college! It was a lot of fun, and I remember that my favorite horse to ride during YEDA was Wyatt, although he wasn't mine yet.

652

Now that I own Wyatt, I can ride him whenever I want! My family and I only live 10 minutes away from Whitney Ridge Stables. We used to live an hour away, but my mom and dad, Erin and Rob, decided we should move closer to the barn since I'm there every day taking care of Wyatt and practicing my classes. My brother, R.J., and my dog, Diesel, really like the extra space to run around in our new yard too.

If my parents drop me off at the barn, sometimes they stay to watch my lesson. Some of the other girls my age at the barn have a family member, a mom or maybe a sister, who also ride, and it's fun for them to share the experience together. But I love having an activity that's all mine, and besides, my mom and dad are both kind of scared of horses!

My **trainers** at Whitney Ridge are Whitney Lagace and Colton LaSusa. They've both won a ton of championships, and they're both really good trainers for the all-around events, especially for **trail**. Whitney owns the barn, and Colton is her business partner.

Since the AQHA holds shows all year round, there's not a beginning or an end of the show season for Whitney and Colton. They are always giving us lessons and training horses that they show themselves or that their **clients** show. They also make sure that all the horses are taken care of and have everything they need like clean **stalls** and **bedding**, **grain**, hay, new **shoes,** and visits from the **veterinarian**. Whitney and Colton also schedule which shows we riders go to and make sure that we have all the equipment we need at the show.

I usually go to the barn every day after school, on the weekends, and even during school vacations. The bus drops me and some of my friends off right at the barn. Although I look after myself at the barn, there are always adults there just in case I need help. Besides Colton and Whitney, usually one of the assistant trainers is at the barn, too.

All the horses have a **paddock** attached to their stall, which is nice for Wyatt to go outside every day. But that means a lot of work for me, especially since his hair is such a light color and he gets really dirty.

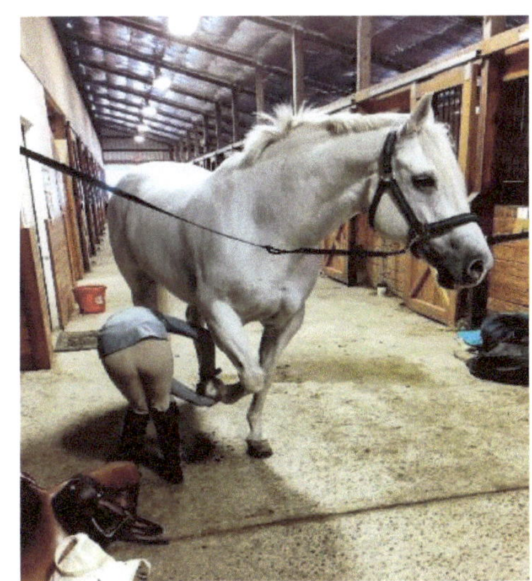

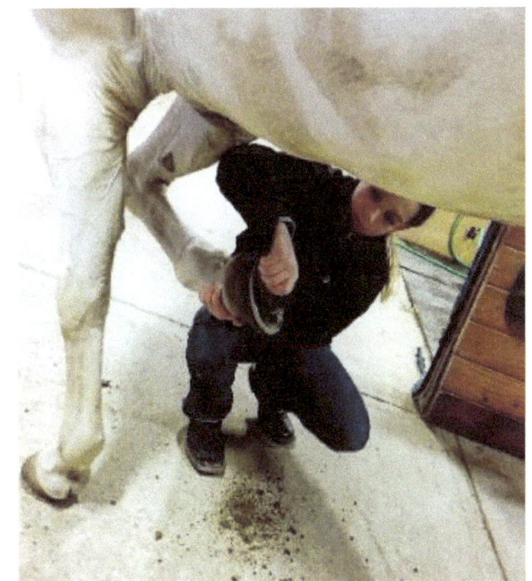

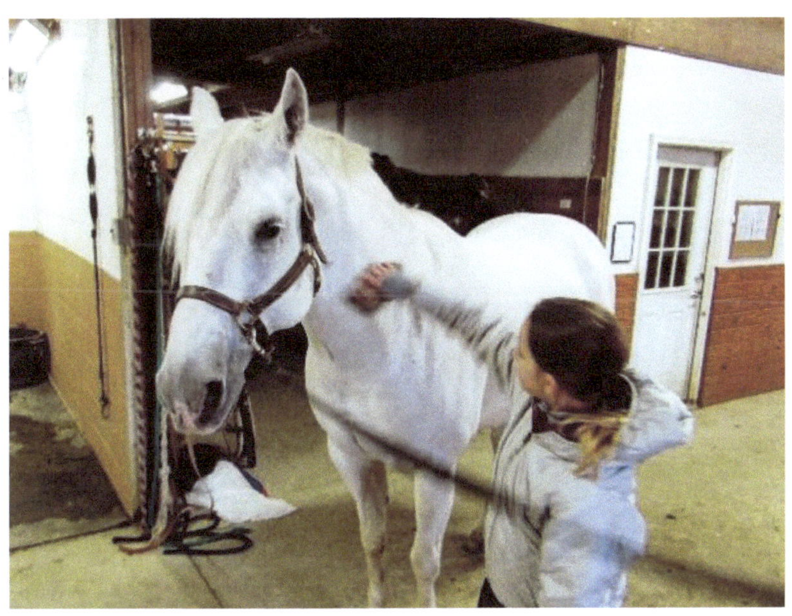

Before I ride, I have to **groom** Wyatt from head to toe by currying him with a **curry comb**, brushing him, and picking out his feet with a **hoof pick**. There is a saying at the barn: "No hoof; no horse." This means that if Wyatt's feet aren't healthy, the rest of this body won't be healthy either. I always make sure to pick his feet out before and after I ride. If he gets a rock stuck in his hoof or if he accidentally cuts his foot, I'll see it and help fix the problem. That's kind of the deal…I take care of him so he can do his best job for me.

Next, I have to lunge him. Even though Wyatt is 17 years old, and that's getting old for a horse, he still has a lot of energy, and I need to lunge him before I ride. I make him **walk**, **trot,** and **canter** in each direction for about 15 minutes total. This gives him a chance to get out some extra energy and have fun before we go to work. If I don't lunge him, he'll be too **fresh,** or frisky, and he won't pay attention to my directions when I ride him.

Next, I put on a **saddle pad** and my saddle. Today, I'm riding western, but sometimes I ride in my English saddle. What saddle I choose depends on what class I want to work on that day. I have different **bridles** for English and western, and they each have different **bits** and **headstalls**. Wyatt and I love riding western, but the saddle is so heavy!

Whitney or Colton usually gives me a lesson or two a week, and then I ride on my own or with some of my friends. There's an indoor **arena** at our barn, and we have an outdoor arena, too. Where I ride depends on the weather outside.

Because I can train both inside and outside, I ride as much as I can no matter the weather. In Connecticut, it can get really hot and humid in the summer, and it can get really cold and windy in the winter. Are there cold days when I might like to snuggle up on the couch and watch a movie instead of freezing my butt off at the barn? Sure! But if I want to be a competitive rider at shows, I know that I have to practice, practice, practice—and that the other kids who I'll be showing against are also working just as hard.

When I ride, I work on my **position** in the saddle, keeping my hands still and quiet while making Wyatt do what I ask without a lot of movement from me. Part of being a good rider is being able to sit properly and having the horse do the things you ask without anyone really noticing. A good rider is constantly making small adjustments with every step the horse takes, even though it looks like you're just sitting there!

I want to ride with my heels down, my chin up, my eyes looking straight ahead, my back straight, and my shoulders, hips, and heels almost in line with each other. It's hard not to look down at your horse when you ride, and I am still working on this skill!

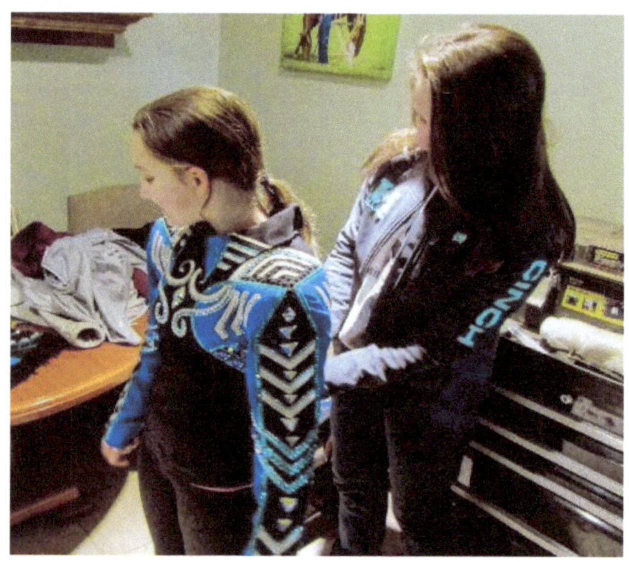

Because this will be my first year showing on the quarter horse circuit, and I have a new horse, I need a new western show outfit. Jayna, Whitney's daughter, is helping me pick out one. Some of the girls at the barn have outgrown their **show clothes**, so I try on a couple of their outfits. Buying their outfits second-hand will be way less expensive than buying brand new clothes! The purple outfit is a little too big, and I don't really like the color.

The blue outfit is perfect and will look great with Wyatt's hair color. There is even a **custom-made** matching saddle pad that will help me and Wyatt look more like a team when we go to our first show. Some people have lots of outfits and pads, but I have just one for now.

In some sports, members of the same team wear identical uniforms and work together to win one prize. But, the AQHA doesn't have any team competitions in the same way that you might if you played soccer or basketball. AQHA showing is very different because each rider competes individually. Even though some people might call the riders from one barn a "show team," every rider who attends the show from the same barn still competes as an individual.

For us riders, a team consists of ourselves and our horse. Wyatt and I need to work together as a team to do well at a show. And even doing well at a show is different from what you might think. For me, doing well at a show means that we performed well in a class or on a piece of a pattern we have been working on—not necessarily winning the class. If we make progress, that's winning!

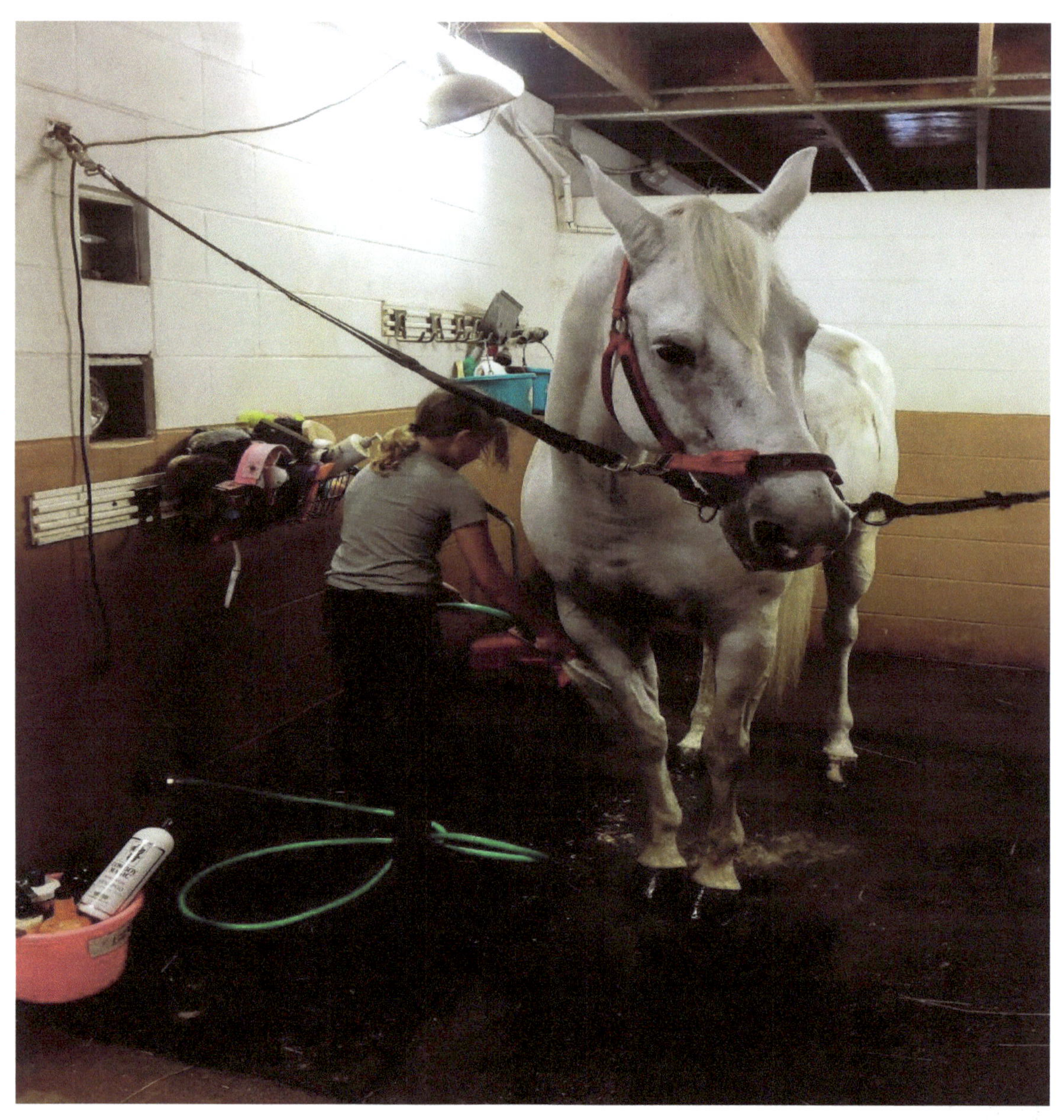

Wyatt gets a bath about once a week, except for when it's really cold in the wintertime. We're lucky to have an indoor **wash rack**!

Wyatt is technically a light grey color, but he looks almost white, and he gets very dirty. I give him a bath before we leave for a show to get most of the dirt off. He'll get lots more baths at a show since he'll be sweaty from working and dirty from laying down in his stall every night. He needs to look spotless when we're in the **show pen**.

Besides bathing Wyatt, I need to make sure my **tack** is clean, too. I use **saddle soap**, a sponge, and some water to clean my bridles and saddles. I also have to scrub the bits on the bridles. Part of making a good presentation at a show is looking good, and a clean horse and clean equipment are part of getting a good score in a class.

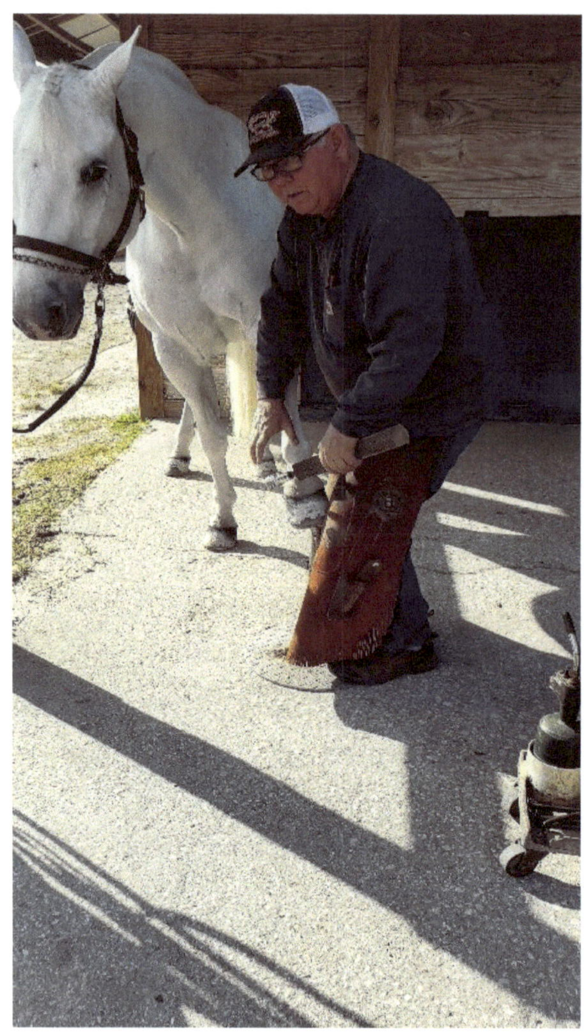

Wyatt also needs to see a **farrier** every five or six weeks so he can perform at his best. The farrier trims Wyatt's feet and puts on four new shoes. Some horses need shoes only on their front feet, but Wyatt is more comfortable with shoes on all four. The farrier first takes off the old shoes by snipping the ends of the nails and then pulling the shoes off with special pliers.

Next, he trims all around Wyatt's feet and shaves off some of the bottom of his **soles** since those areas grow all the time, just like fingernails. If Wyatt's feet get too long, he gets sore, and he might even trip!

The farrier shapes the new shoes to fit each of Wyatt's hooves properly, and then, he nails them on to the bottom of each hoof. A horse's hoof doesn't have any feeling unless the nail goes in the wrong place, so the farrier needs to be both knowledgeable about a horse's body and accurate when nailing on new shoes.

The final step for positioning new shoes is to **rasp** the extra bits of Wyatt's hoof around the edge of the shoe, like when you cut the edges off a pie crust after you put crust on top of the pie.

Even though I'm pretty busy when I'm at the barn, I always have time for some fun. My friend Olivia and I are best friends, and we like to hang out together with our horses. We're both very serious about riding, and we love going to shows most of all.

It's also really nice having Wyatt to talk to sometimes. He's a good listener when I'm mad or upset, and he always takes my side…or at least I like to think that he does!

When it's time to go to a show, Whitney and Colton spring into action! They let us know when and where the shows are located, and they also make sure that the horses and supplies are ready to go!

Whitney and Colton drive all of the horses to the show in two separate trailers. Each trailer can hold several horses, and there is a lot of storage in the trailers, too. The horses are used to riding in the trailers, and they like to travel because they can eat as much hay as they want! If it's a very long trip, sometimes Whitney and Colton will take a break from driving and spend the night at a horse hotel, but most of the time, Whitney and Colton will drive straight through to the show. Horses can sleep standing up, so they don't mind standing in the trailers for long periods of time.

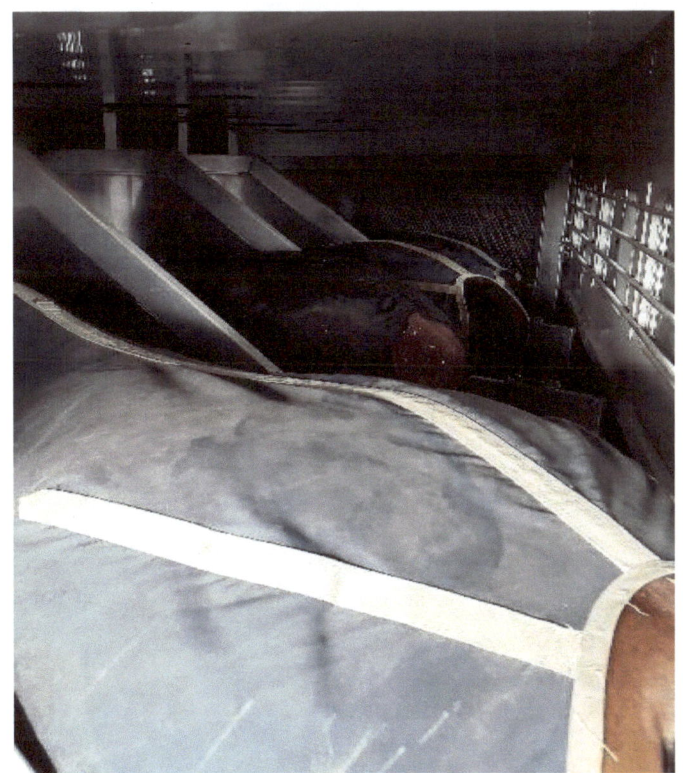

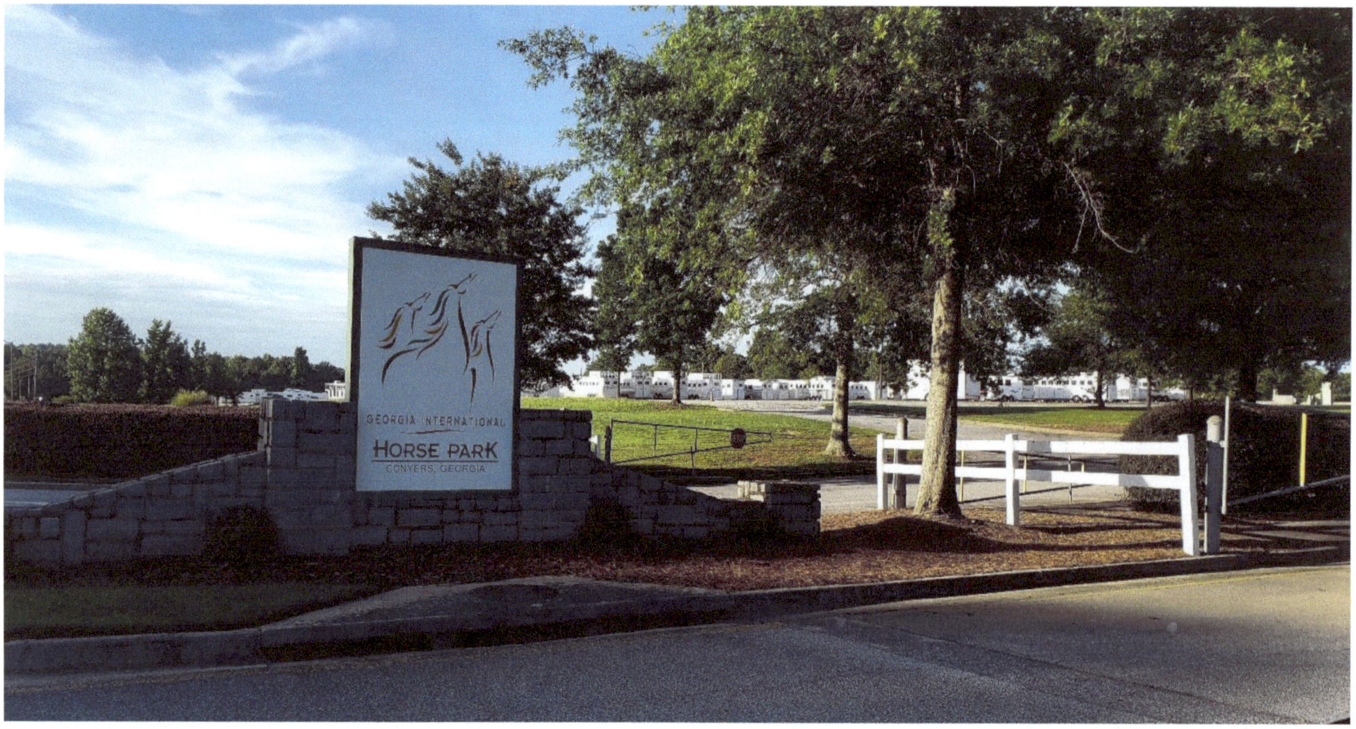
GEORGIA INTERNATIONAL
HORSE PARK
CONYERS, GEORGIA

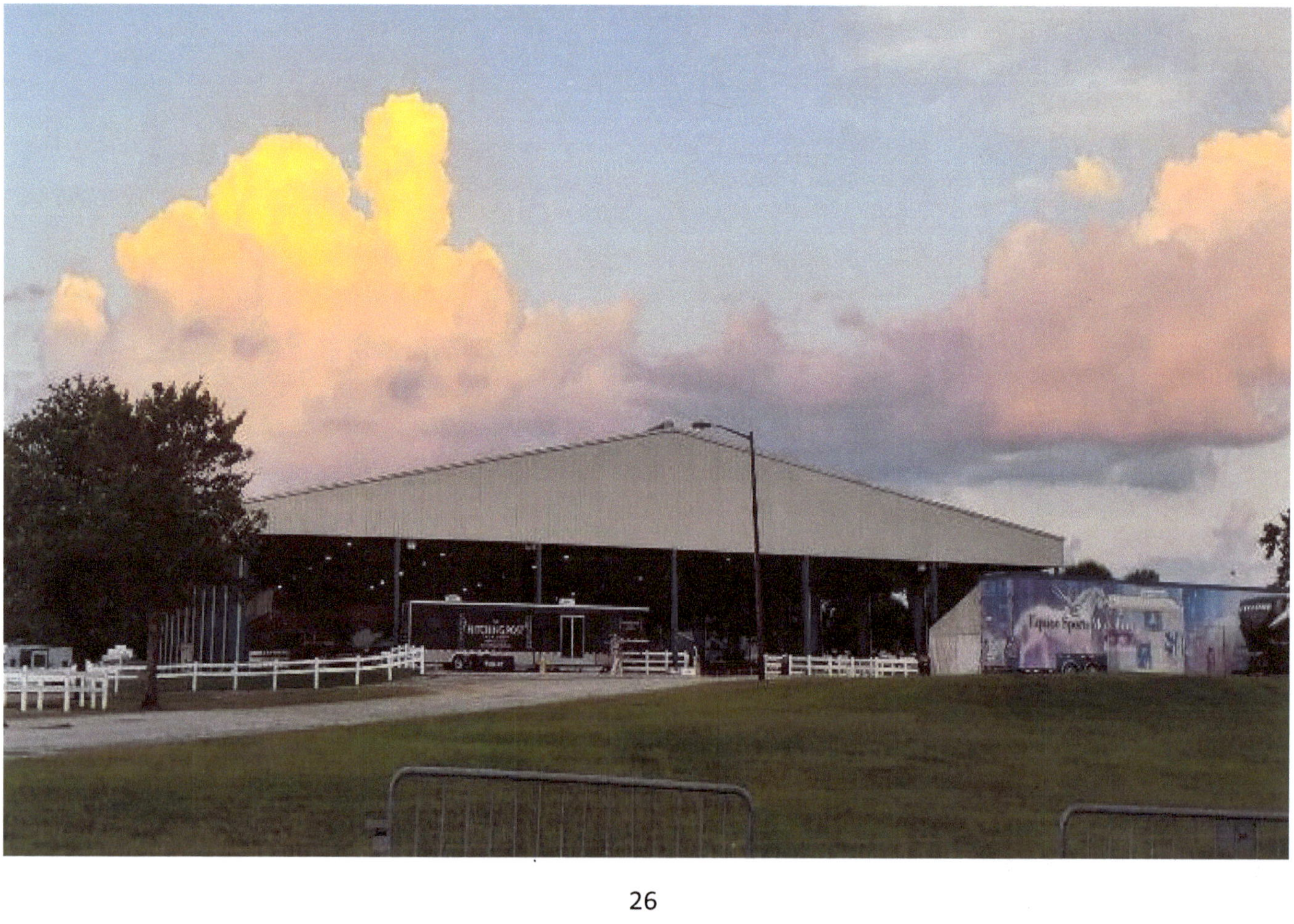

We go to AQHA shows on the East Coast because they are close to home. My favorite shows are in Georgia and Florida. The Georgia AQHA show is held at the same place where they held the 1996 Summer Olympics in Atlanta. The show grounds are amazing!

Each show lasts for one to two weeks! The days feel very long because we are constantly showing and taking care of our horses. For most of the shows I'll be going to this year, four of us kids from Whitney's barn will be showing. Jayna, Ashley, Olivia, and I usually drive to the shows with some other people from the barn in the camper that Whitney owns. We sleep in the bunk beds in the back of camper, and we always have a good time.

My favorite part of staying in the camper is trying out my cooking skills. I love to make brookies, which are brownie cookies, and ramen noodles!

If we go to shows during the school year, we have to go to virtual classes and do our homework to keep up with the other kids in our class. That's a very important part of being on the Whitney Ridge Stables show team: You have to be a good student and do your homework while at the show. Otherwise, if you decide to skip class or an assignment, you won't be allowed to go to the shows during the school year.

At a show, we have three equipment stalls, and each one has its own organization system. One stall holds saddles and bridles, one stall stores show clothes for everyone from our barn, and the last one has saddle pads, tails, and other miscellaneous things we need.

All of the horses who show in AQHA all-around shows wear fake tails, even if their own tails are naturally bushy. Wearing fake tails makes all of the horses' tails the same length and gives them a polished look.

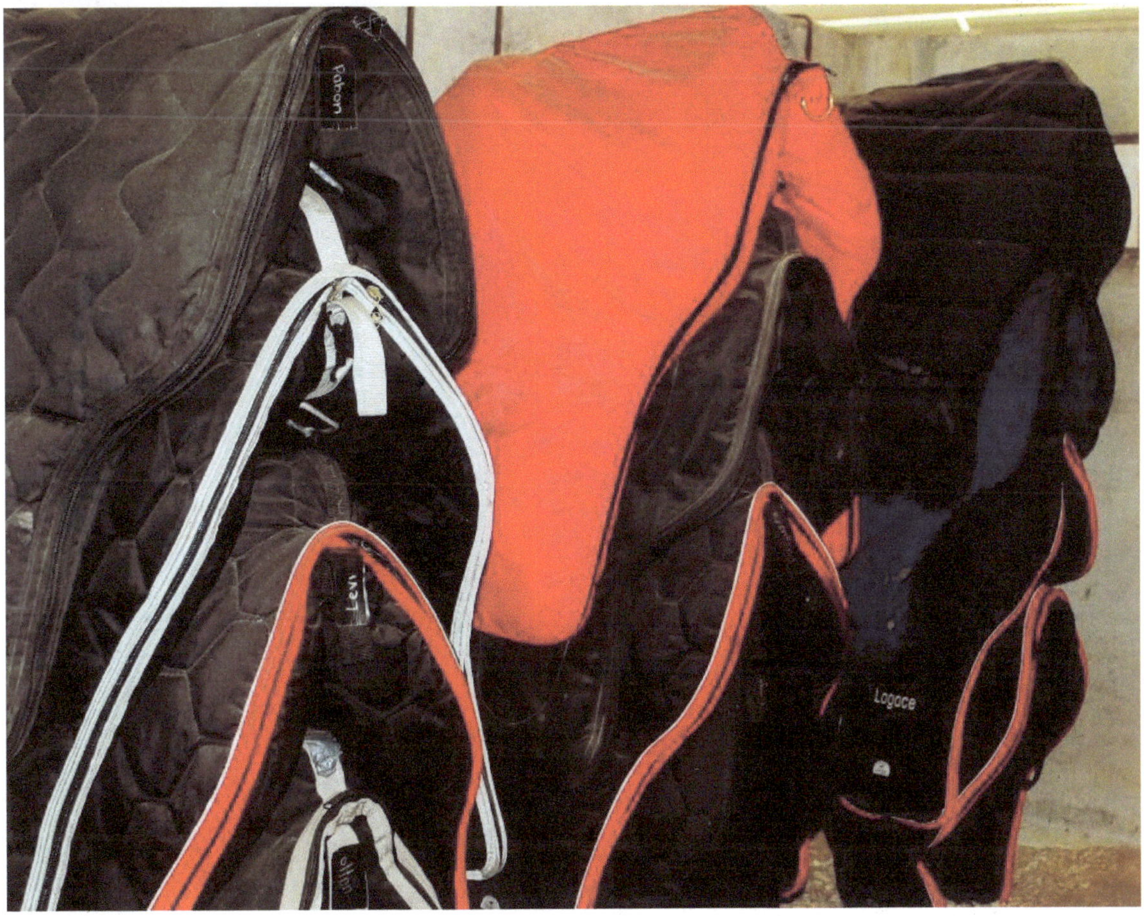

My show day starts pretty early in the morning. After the crew is finished watering and dragging the show pens to make them smooth and not too dusty, I lunge Wyatt for at least a half an hour. I don't know why such an old horse needs so much exercise, but he sure does!

Then I **lope** him for another half an hour or so, and finally he starts to settle down and actually listen to me! Now I know he's ready to show. Once or twice at past shows, I skipped riding or lunging Wyatt in the morning, and when I went into a class later that day, it was a disaster. Wyatt wouldn't listen, or I got flustered, or both, so I've learned that getting up early and preparing my horse properly makes for a successful ride.

Anyone at a show can get flustered, though. Sometimes I do a better job than Wyatt in a class, and sometimes I'm the one who lets him down. I think Wyatt wants to win and do well, and I feel bad if I mess up on a skill I should know how to do. Sometimes I even forget my patterns, which is embarrassing! It's frustrating to practice for months at the barn and then make a mistake or have your horse not cooperate at the show, but that's the way it goes. Everyone has good days and bad days.

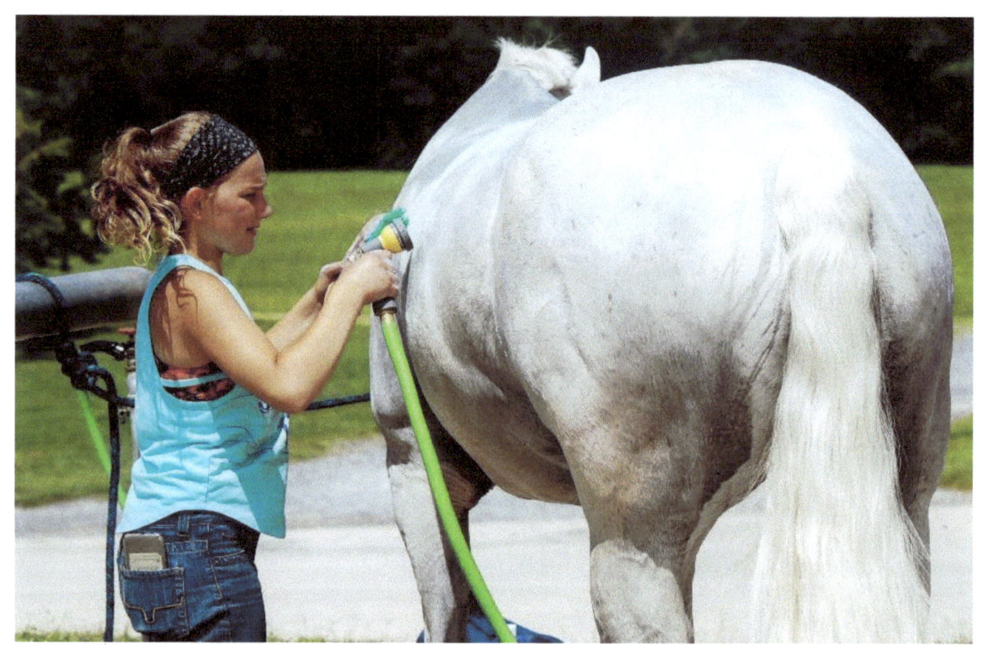

Next, Wyatt gets a bath…again! He is always dirty from the night before, and he needs to be clean and show-ready every day. I even have to wash his fake tail, his real tail, and his **mane**. Wyatt's mane needs to be clean because a professional braider comes around to our stalls to **braid** or **band** our horses' manes. His hairdo will stay in for days at the show because it's part of making him show-ready.

While Wyatt is drying off from his bath and I'm waiting for my classes to start, I escape with Olivia on our **Segways** for a quick bite to eat. We love having the Segways instead of bikes because we can carry things in our hands while we ride. Plus, they are easy to pack in the trailer and don't take up much space when we travel to shows. Bikes are much bigger and heavier to transport!

At this show, Olivia had to get her cowboy hat reshaped, so we picked that up at the hat vendor along the way. Sometimes cowboy hats get a bit floppy over time, and they need to be reshaped to look perky and sharp again. To help them keep their shape, we store the hats in a hat carrier—and hers is a cool blue color.

Finally, it's time to get into my show clothes and get Wyatt ready for my classes. For the western classes, I wear **chaps**: leather pants with lots of fringe and long zippers. They fit really snugly, and most of us can't get them on without help because they are really long and hang down over your boots once you're on your horse. This makes the chaps really hard to walk in, so I always fold my cuffs over until I'm up on Wyatt.

After I get dressed, it's time for hair and make-up. I wear my hair in different styles depending on the class in which I'm showing. I wear a ponytail for **trail**, **pleasure,** and **western riding.** My hair is in a tight bun for all my English classes and western **horsemanship**. I only wear a little bit of make-up and some lip gloss. I don't really like putting on make-up, but it's all part of looking good in the show pen.

Every person who shows is assigned a number to help the judges and the audience know who each rider and horse is in the show pen. I have to wear my numbers on both sides of my saddle pad. If I forget one or both numbers, I'll be disqualified—which is not good! I always double check that the numbers are secure to the pad, and then I'm off to the show pen where I'll meet Whitney or Colton for last minute instructions.

As I approach the pen, I see the chairman of the AQHA Professional Horsemen's Association and nationally known trainer, Gene "Geno" Spagnola. He's being interviewed for the online show *Keeping It Real*. Before I even started riding, Geno showed Wyatt at the AQHA World Show and did really well with him! Sometimes when I see him at shows, he comes over and visits with me and Wyatt before our classes.

I'd love to show at the AQHA Youth World Show someday. Jayna has been to it a bunch of times, and I'm hoping with more practice and show experience, I can qualify to go one day, too.

679

679

My first classes to compete in today are trail classes. Of course, I get a few pointers from Colton before the class starts. I like a little encouragement from my coaches, and they're both very good at talking me through the patterns. Sometimes I get a little nervous before I compete. It helps to have my coaches remind me about the tricky parts of the pattern and to assure me that I'm well prepared for the class.

I think that in a lot of sports, you can learn all the skills you need to succeed, but if you don't feel confident, you may not perform your best. When you have a partner—like Wyatt—who doesn't understand words, it's even more important to have confidence because he senses how I'm feeling and feeds off that. So, if I'm scared, he'll be scared, but if I'm strong, he'll be strong. Horses are so smart!

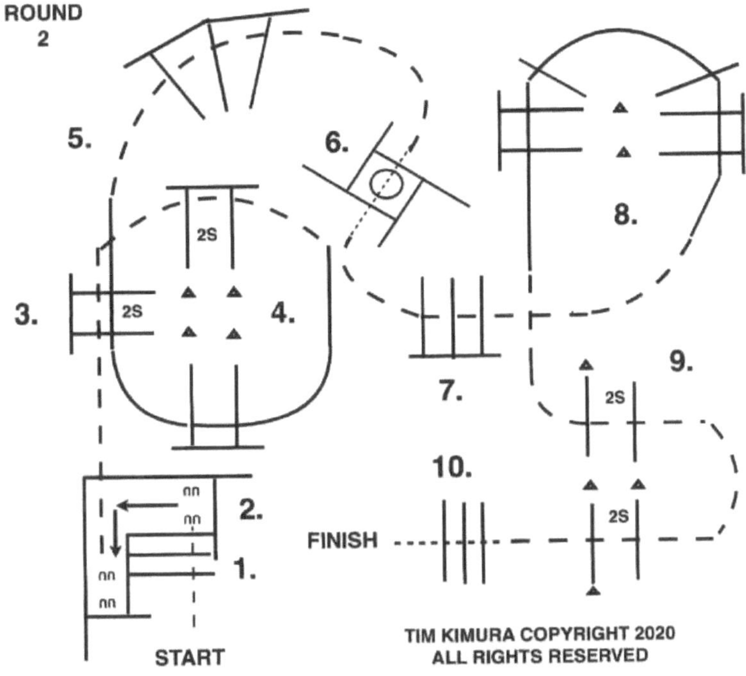

1. JOG OVER POLES, JOG INTO CHUTE AND STOP.
2. SIDE PASS LEFT, THEN BACK INTO CHUTE.
3. JOG OUT CHUTE, JOG OVER POLES.
4. LOPE OVER POLES (RIGHT LEAD).
5. BREAK TO THE JOG, JOG OVER POLES.
6. STOP OR BREAK TO THE WALK, WALK INTO BOX, EXECUTE A 360 TURN EITHER WAY, WALK OUT BOX.
7. JOG OVER POLES.
8. LOPE OVER POLES (LEFT LEAD).
9. BREAK TO THE JOG, JOG OVER POLES.
10. STOP OR BREAK TO THE WALK, WALK OVER POLES.

Trail class has a lot of obstacles that you have to do at a certain **gait** in a certain pattern. The trail patterns change for every show, and we get to practice the patterns the night before. There are always lope-overs, a back-through, a side pass where the horse moves sideways, some **jog**-overs, and sometimes a gate or even a small bridge to walk over.

In today's pattern, there are lots of pinwheels to jog and lope over, so placing my horse in just the right spot is very important. The riders can see the patterns online a few days before the competition day. Wyatt and I practiced the pattern last night, which makes me feel more confident that we can ride well today.

289

I compete in the novice youth class. This class is for kids under age 18 who haven't earned enough points in all of their showing to have qualified out of the novice **division** yet. And I also compete in the 13 and under division for any ability rider under 13 years old. Even though the other kids are pretty good riders and have been competing their whole lives, Wyatt has been showing for a long time, and he helps me through the classes. After showing for many years, horses get to know where they're supposed to put their feet, so Wyatt sometimes knows more than I do about trail!

IN YOUR CAR

Between classes, Olivia and I check out the show grounds. There are vendors who sell show clothing, horse equipment, hats, and of course, lots of food. I'm a vegetarian so sometimes it's a challenge to find food that I can eat. I absolutely love pizza and macaroni and cheese, and I can usually find that at horse shows. We also bring a lot of food in the camper for all of us to share during the two weeks we are at the show.

We like to go to the Harris Saddlery trailer and look at all the new saddles and headstalls. This vendor always has some really nice tack and equipment, and you can even get a custom-made saddle with your name or initials. I like the saddles that are made with more than one color of leather.

Sometimes we go and check out the vendors who sell other clothes, supplies, and equipment, even if we don't need anything. I love looking at all the colors of the fake tails and the new show clothes, too. The outfits are always super sparkly, but some of the jackets have so many gemstones which make them really heavy to wear. These outfits look great in the show pen, but when you're showing, it feels like it weighs a ton!

It's always fun at a show like this because we usually have a golf cart to ride around on, too. Sometimes Whitney gets mad at us for taking it because it's supposed to be her cart. She usually only gets mad when she needs it and can't find it. Oops!

Tonight there's an event called Show for Dough which is a special trail class in which the riders pay an extra entry fee and can win prize money if they do well. This class takes place in the same arena where they held the big show jumping during the 1996 Summer Olympics. Tonight's trail pattern is very challenging, and only the most experienced riders usually compete.

We all go to watch Whitney and Colton compete, and there is free food and drinks, too! It's my goal to compete in the Show for Dough class someday, but I've got a lot of work to do before I get there.

Sometimes we go out to eat at a local restaurant with a group of friends from other barns. It's hard to organize because everyone has different show schedules and practice times, but when we can all go for lunch or dinner, it's a fun way to catch up and meet new friends.

My friend, Carly, is from Vermont and rides at Geno's barn so we see her a lot. She's in a different division from me so we don't compete against each other.

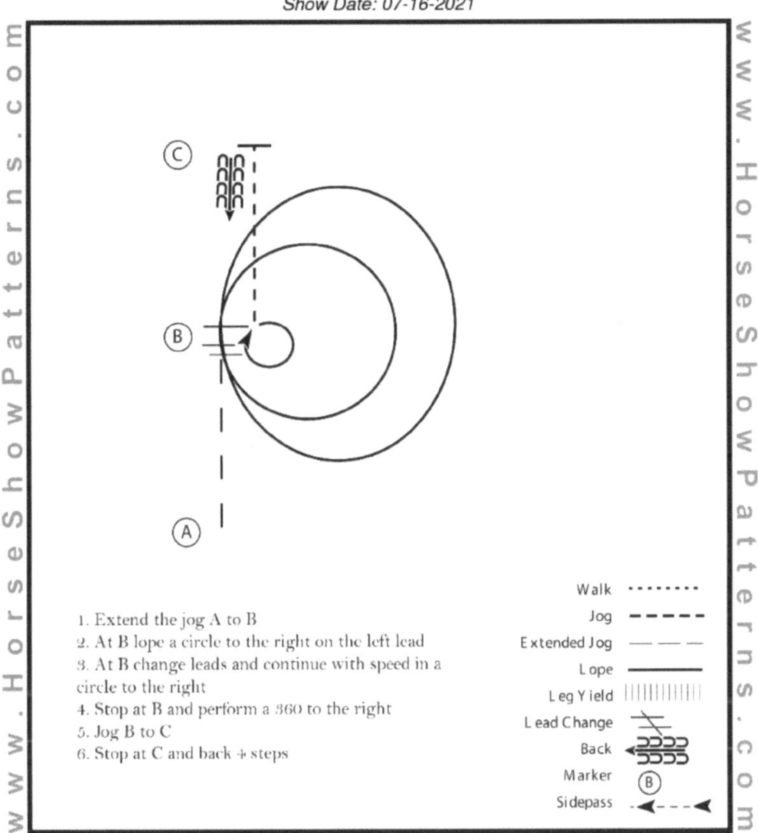

The next day, I prepare for another one of my classes: horsemanship. In this western class, you and your horse perform a very specific pattern. The judges are looking for how well you completed the pattern, how well you controlled your horse, and how good your body position was throughout the pattern. I really like horsemanship, and Wyatt and I can be successful if we lay the pattern out correctly and complete the skills at the exact spot that we're supposed to.

Like trail, the horsemanship patterns change at every show, but they usually have some of the same parts like walk, jog, lope, back, and turn. Since I can see the horsemanship pattern online a few days ahead of time, I like to practice each piece of the pattern before the class.

We don't usually complete the whole pattern from beginning to end in practice because Wyatt is very smart, and he will anticipate what he's supposed to do next before I even ask him! But it's still good to go over each piece and get it right in practice.

In the horsemanship class, each rider completes the pattern one at a time. After all of the riders are finished, everyone goes back to ride on the **rail** at all three gaits: for western, it's the walk, jog, and lope. Sometimes we line up for the **placings,** but most of the time, we leave the ring, and they announce the placings over the loudspeaker. Whitney always makes time to talk to me about how the class went overall, discussing what went well and what I still need to work on.

Once in a while, a horse will get sick or hurt or just not feel well at a show. We think Wyatt might have a little stomachache called **colic**. So, I take him over to the veterinarian trailer to get checked out. The vet needs to be properly trained and skilled at quickly diagnosing the horse's health problems. It turns out that Wyatt is just a bit dehydrated, so the vet and his team give him some fluids through an IV needle in his neck. We both get the day off while Wyatt rests and recuperates.

The next day, Wyatt is feeling much better, and we have hunt seat or English **equitation**. It's kind of like horsemanship, but the gaits are a little different, and you use English tack and clothing. In the English classes, we all look alike because there's not much variety in the clothing. We wear black boots, tan breeches, a black hunt cap, white shirt, and either a navy or black jacket. The western outfits are much more sparkly and colorful. There are definitely more interesting styles of what you can wear showing in western classes!

Hunt Seat Equitation (13&Under, 14-18, Amateur and Select)

Show Date: 07-16-2021

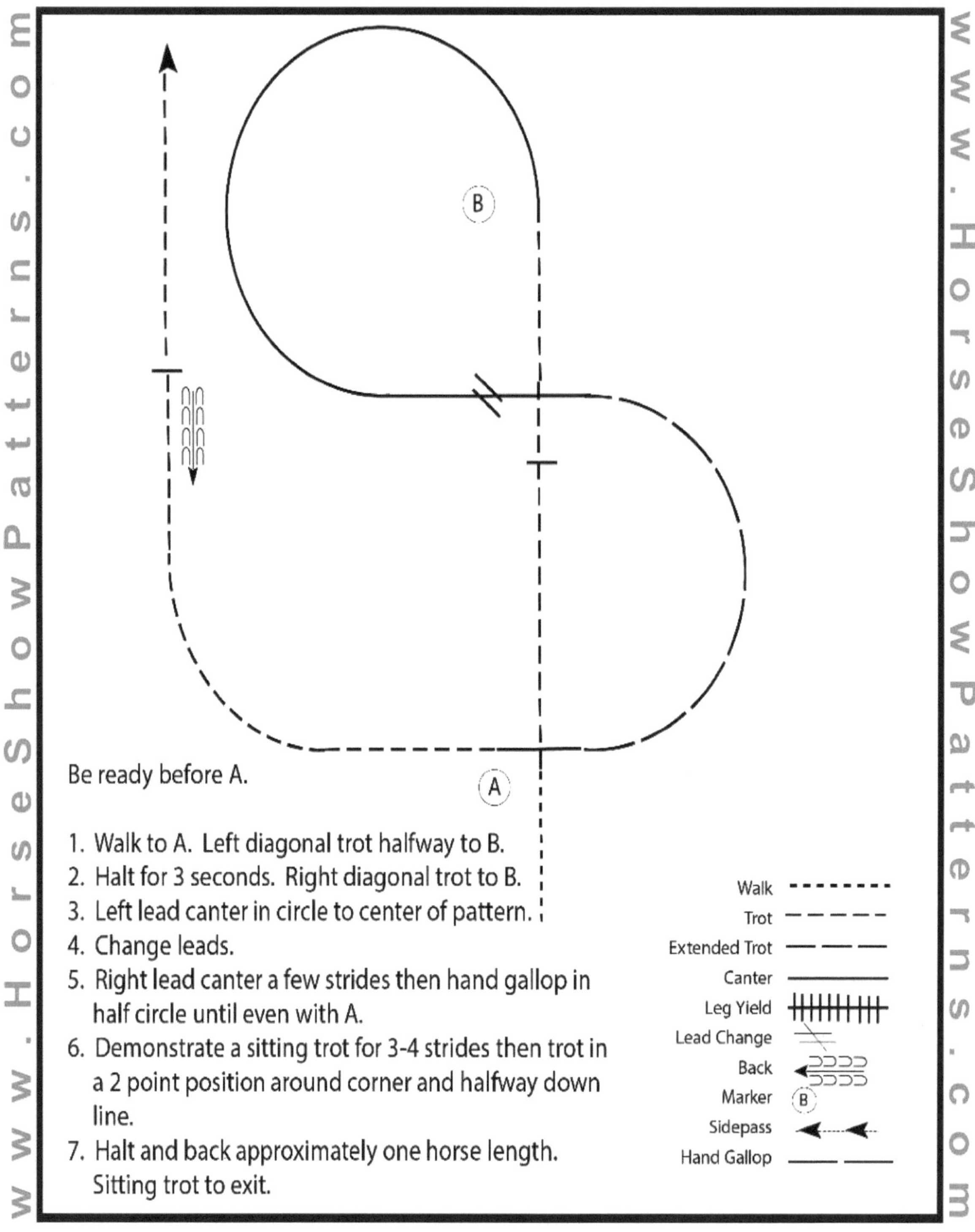

There are patterns in the equitation just like in the horsemanship, and similarly, it's judged on my position in the saddle and how well Wyatt and I can perform the pattern. Instead of walk, jog, and lope, the gaits for the equitation are walk, trot, canter, and **hand gallop**, which is similar to the western but much more **forward** and with longer strides. I also have to **post** at the trot, which is when you rise and fall with each step at the trot. Posting makes it easier to ride the trot because it can be very bouncy! After the pattern, we do rail work just like in the horsemanship.

Jayna competes in a class called **showmanship**. Most people who are competing for the all-around high point award compete in this class. I would participate too, but Wyatt sometimes nips me when I'm leading him. It's a bad habit that's hard to break, but luckily, he doesn't use his teeth, just his lips. Still, it's not a good thing, and I'd get disqualified if he did it in a class.

In showmanship, you don't ride the horse. You lead the horse through a pattern and have to walk, trot, turn, back, and set up for **inspection**. It sounds easy, but it's one of the most difficult classes to do well because it has to look like you're almost dancing with your horse. Each step needs to be in sync, and you can't pull on your horse at all. The horse needs to follow very slight **cues** from your hand and watch your body position so he'll know where and when to go.

Whitney's friend, Gretchen Mathes who is Geno's business partner, is a long-time AQHA judge and trains horses in Connecticut, too. She is great at teaching showmanship to both horses and competitors. Sometimes when she's not judging at the show, Gretchen gives Jayna some tips on this class.

Besides trail, horsemanship, and equitation, I also compete in a **halter class**, a western pleasure class, a western riding class, and a hunter under saddle class. There are even more types of classes that I don't participate in like reining, jumping, and even **barrel racing**. You have to compete in several different kinds of classes to qualify as an all-around rider, not just one or two classes.

No. of entries in class	1st	2nd	3rd	4th	5th	6th	7th	8th	9th	10th
3-4	1/2									
5-9	1	1/2								
10-14	2	1	1/2							
15-19	3	2	1	1/2						
20-24	4	3	2	1	1/2					
25-29	5	4	3	2	1	1/2				
30-34	6	5	4	3	2	1	1/2			
35-39	7	6	5	4	3	2	1	1/2		
40-44	8	7	6	5	4	3	2	1	1/2	
45 & more	9	8	7	6	5	4	3	2	1	1/2

At the end of a show, there are awards for the all-around high-point rider in each division. That means that all of my points from placings get added up together at the end of the show. You get points depending on where you place within a class and how many people were in the class. You get more points if you place well in a large class compared to placing well in a small class.

Sometimes after adding up all of my points, I win either champion, or first place, or reserve champion, which is second place, in my division. If I do win, I get a cool prize like a blanket for my horse or even a belt buckle.

If you win one of these awards at a big show, it's fun to have a **backdrop** picture taken by a professional photographer. The finished product looks great, but there's a lot of work that goes into getting just the right shot. The first thing that's hard is actually getting everyone together in one spot at the same time! The photographer's assistant sets Wyatt's feet just right and lines up the other people who will be in the picture, too.

Once Whitney, Olivia, and Jayna are lined up, the assistant uses a broom or sometimes a stuffed hobby horse to get Wyatt's attention, so he'll put his ears up. We have to keep smiling the whole time while the photographer takes about 20 pictures, hoping one of them will be good of all of us. It's quite a process, but usually the picture turns out great!

Perfect! At the show, the backdrop is a solid blue color, but after we take the picture, the photographer can digitally add extra designs, signs, and show logos. They can even add in any prizes that you won like a saddle, a trophy, or a jacket. These pictures are a fun way to celebrate our hard work and commemorate a great show.

It all looks like so much fun, right? Well, here are a few more things that people who don't show horses wouldn't know. In fact, most people think riding and showing is easy. But it's not.

Most people don't see all the tiny cues I'm giving my horse every single step of the way. They don't see the frustration when Wyatt or I just can't seem to get it right, over and over again. Or the times that I think I'm prepared for a class and then I forget just one piece of the pattern and I'm out of the competition. Or the times when I really want to be happy for Jayna or Olivia when they place high in a class, but I'm so disappointed because I didn't do well. Or even the times when I get scared and want to get off Wyatt, but the trainer makes me work through a rough part.

It's hard to be a good rider. You have to be mentally tough when sometimes you just want to scream or cry. You have to be humble when you do well, even though you might want to excitedly shout out loud that you just had a fantastic pattern. I guess it's the same with lots of sports, but for people who show horses, it's not only your mind and thoughts you have to manage but your horse's as well.

Maybe that's why it's so exhilarating. We don't get much for prizes or awards given out at the shows. What we do get is the satisfaction of working with a living animal who has limited communication and knowing that we've both done our absolute best—and everyday our best gets a little bit better than the day before.

Well, it's back to the stalls for us. I can't wait for the next show, and I know Wyatt and I will have many more adventures ahead of us.

I hope you've enjoyed learning more about being an all-around rider—and a bit about having a horse, too! Maybe I'll see you soon at an AQHA all-around competition, and make sure to come and say hi to me and Wyatt!

Glossary

all-around when a rider competes in many types of classes, usually both English and western.

arena a large flat space with soft footing used for riding and exercising a horse. There are both indoor and outdoor arenas.

backdrop a fancy background used in a professional photograph.

band the way a horse's mane is styled for western classes with small ponytails all along the neck.

barn name the name you call your horse at home instead of his or her registered name at the show.

barrel racing a class where a horse and rider complete a pattern around three barrels. The winner completes the pattern in the shortest amount of time.

bedding the material you put in a horse's stall, usually wood shavings, sawdust, or straw.

bit the metal piece that goes in a horse's mouth when you're riding.

braid the way a horse's mane is styled for English classes with short braids tied up tight to the neck.

breed the type of horse you have based on the genetics of the horse's parents.

bridle the equipment the horse wears on its head when you're riding, including a headstall, bit, and reins.

canter a medium-fast English gait with three beats and either a right lead or a left lead designation.

chaps leather or suede pants worn over trousers, usually decorated with studs or fringe. Chaps are worn when competing in western classes.

circuit shows or classes on multiple days in the same location.

client a rider who pays for the services of a professional trainer.

cue signals you give to your horse with your body, voice, legs, and hands to ask the horse to do different things.

curry comb a rubber tool with circular ridges used to loosen and lift dirt off a horse's coat.

custom-made a piece of equipment or clothing that is made especially for you or your horse.

cutting a western discipline when a rider and horse separate one cow out of a herd and keep it from returning to the herd by moving quickly left and right as the cow tries to get back.

discipline the events or classes you specialize in.

division the level of a class you can compete in. The division usually depends on your age or the level of riding accomplishment you've reached.

dressage an English discipline of riding a specific pattern consisting of a walk, trot, and canter and extensions of each. There are more difficult maneuvers at higher dressage levels.

driving a discipline where a driver steers a horse pulling a cart or buggy.

English a style of riding defined by the tack and equipment used and the way a horse moves on the arena, including jumping, dressage, equitation, and hunter under saddle.

equitation an English class that is judged on how well a rider maintains an excellent position while maneuvering their horse through a specific pattern.

farrier someone who specializes in caring for a horse's feet by trimming and shoeing the horse.

forward moving a bit faster than normal in a gait.

fresh a horse's behavior when it has too much energy or isn't paying attention to its rider.

gait the way a horse moves at different speeds, including walk, trot/jog, canter/lope, and hand gallop.

grain what a horse eats, usually oats, corn, and wheat.

groom keeping your horse healthy and clean by washing, currying, brushing, picking feet, and combing mane and tail.

halter class a class where a horse is led by a handler and is judged on its conformation, or its appearance.

hand gallop a controlled English gait that is faster than a canter and is used for jumping and equitation patterns.

headstall the leather part of a bridle not including the reins.

hoof pick the tool used to clean a horse's feet.

horsemanship a western class that is judged on how well a rider maintains an excellent position while maneuvering their horse through a specific pattern.

hunter under saddle an English discipline judged mostly on the horse's way of moving and consistency through the walk, trot, and canter.

Generally, bigger horses are used in this discipline because of their long, low strides.

inspection when a judge walks around your horse in showmanship class, checking to see that you are showing your horse at its best.

jog a slow western gait with two beats, and diagonal legs that move at the same time.

lead at the canter or lope, you're on either right lead or left lead which is determined by which front foot of the horse goes forward the most

lope a medium western gait with three beats and either a right lead or a left lead designation.

lunge exercising your horse in an arena. The horse is on a long line and moves in a circle around you.

mane the long hair that grows out of the top of a horse's neck.

novice the beginner division.

open classes that anyone can enter, usually containing the best horses and riders, including trainers.

paddock a small enclosure for a horse to go outside, sometimes attached to the stall.

placings a rider's ranking in a class as determined by a judge.

position how you hold your body, arms, legs, and head when you ride on the horse.

post the up-and-down movement used by a rider at a trot to make the ride smoother for both the rider and horse.

rail or rail work when you ride around the edge of the arena.

rasp a tool used by a farrier to file off parts of the hoof.

regional the area of the country you live in, as well as the nearby states.

registered an official record of your horse's name, birthday, and family tree or pedigree.

reining a western discipline when the horse and rider complete a specific pattern of circles, spins, and sliding stops at a lope and gallop.

saddle pad the cushioning that goes in between your saddle and your horse.

saddle soap special soap used just for cleaning leather.

Segway an electric two-wheeled device that you ride on and steer with your feet.

show clothes the outfit you wear specifically when you're showing your horse.

show pen an arena used for show classes.

showmanship a class where a horse is led by the handler through a specific pattern that includes walk, trot, back, and turn.

sole the flat part of the bottom of a horse's hoof.

stall where a horse lives in a barn. Sometimes, stalls also refer to the vendor booths at shows.

tack the equipment you use to ride your horse that you actually put on your horse.

thoroughbred a breed that is often crossed with a quarter horse resulting in an Appendix Quarter Horse.

trainer an expert who works with you or your horse.

trot a medium English gait with two beats, and diagonal legs that move at the same time.

veterinarian an animal doctor.

walk the slowest gait that has four beats.

wash rack a safe place to tie your horse when giving it a bath, complete with a water hose and drainage area. Wash racks can be outside or inside.

western a style of riding defined by the tack and equipment used and the way a horse moves on the arena, including trail, horsemanship, pleasure, reining, speed events, ranch riding, and all livestock-related events.

western pleasure a western discipline judged mostly on the horse's way of moving and consistency through the walk, jog, and lope. Generally, a slow gait and a loose rein are desired in this discipline.

western riding a pattern class ridden mostly at the lope involving lots of serpentines and lead changes and is judged on consistency of speed and quality of the horse's movement.

Photo Acknowledgements

All photographs that appear in this book were taken by Jill Thomas unless otherwise noted below.

Cover – Sarah Rosciti, SR Images
2-3 – Erin Ortega
4-5 – Shane Rux Photography
6-7 – Erin Ortega
10-18 – Erin Ortega
22 – Erin Ortega
28 – Whitney Lagace
41 – Pattern by Tim Kimura
53 – Pattern by HorseShowPatterns.com
60 – Pattern by HorseShowPatterns.com
64 – Shane Rux Photography
68 – Cody Parmenter Photography
78 – Bryan Nigro Photography

About the Author

Jill Thomas lives and works in Vermont with her husband, Jeff, and three dogs. She shows her American Quarter Horse, Its Al Ways Sumthing "Chichi," in the all-around classes at many of the shows on the East Coast. Jill is also a real estate investor who flips houses in Arizona, New Hampshire, and Vermont. She is planning the next book in the Quarter Horse Kids series, A Barrel Racer.

www.ingramcontent.com/pod-product-compliance
Lightning Source LLC
LaVergne TN
LVHW070138110826
845147LV00002B/282
* 9 7 9 8 9 8 5 3 7 3 3 0 1 *